18.92

Profiles in Greek and Roman Mythology

HEPHAESTUS

Mitchell Lane
PUBLISHERS
P.O. Box 196
Hockessin, Delaware 19707
Visit us on the web: www.mitchelllane.com
Comments? email us: mitchelllane@mitchelllane.com

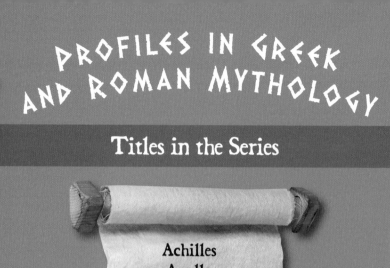

PROFILES IN GREEK AND ROMAN MYTHOLOGY

Titles in the Series

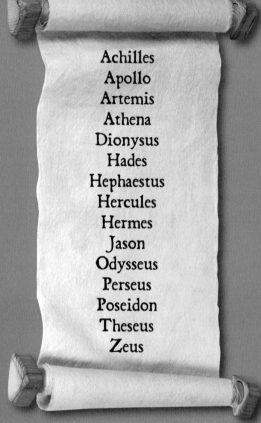

Profiles in Greek and Roman Mythology

HEPHAESTUS

Kayleen Reusser

Mitchell Lane
PUBLISHERS
P.O. Box 196
Hockessin, Delaware 19707
Visit us on the web: www.mitchelllane.com
Comments? email us: mitchelllane@mitchelllane.com

Mitchell Lane

PUBLISHERS

Copyright © 2010 by Mitchell Lane Publishers. All rights reserved. No part of this book may be reproduced without written permission from the publisher. Printed and bound in the United States of America.

Printing   1   2   3   4   5   6   7   8   9

Library of Congress Cataloging-in-Publication Data
Reusser, Kayleen.
  Hephaestus / by Kayleen Reusser.
      p. cm.—(Profiles in Greek and Roman mythology)
  Includes bibliographical references (p.   ) and index.
  ISBN 978-1-58415-749-6 (library bound)
  I. Hephaestus (Greek deity)—Juvenile literature. I. Title.
  BL820.V8R48 2010
  398.20938'01—dc22
                                                                    2009045665

ABOUT THE AUTHOR: Kayleen Reusser has written several children's books, including Blue Banner biographies for Mitchell Lane on Selena Gomez, Leona Lewis, and Taylor Swift. She is also the author of *Hermes* and *Hades* in this series. She learns about children's reading interests by working in a middle school library. Reusser lives with her family in the Midwest.

AUTHOR'S NOTE: The stories retold in this book use dialog as an aid to readability. The dialog is based on the author's research.

PUBLISHER'S NOTE: This story is based on the author's extensive research, which she believes to be accurate. Documentation of such research is contained on page 46.

The internet sites referenced herein were active as of the publication date. Due to the fleeting nature of some web sites, we cannot guarantee they will all be active when you are reading this book.

To reflect current usage, we have chosen to use the secular era designations BCE ("before the common era") and CE ("of the common era") instead of the traditional designations BC ("before Christ") and AD (*anno Domini*, "in the year of the Lord").

TABLE OF CONTENTS

Profiles in Greek and Roman Mythology

HEPHAESTUS

Peter Paul Rubens painted *Vulcan Forging the Lightning of Jupiter* in the seventeenth century. Hephaestus, the Greek god of the forge, was known as Vulcan to the Romans. One of his most important tasks was fashioning lightning bolts for Zeus (Jupiter).

HEPHAESTUS

With a deafening clang, the heavy hammer slammed against the fiery-hot anvil, creating sparks in the blackened cave. Bent low over his work, Hephaestus (heh-FES-tus) barely noticed the raucous noise. Day after day, he stood at the forge, heating metal in the flames until it glowed red, orange, yellow, and finally white. At that stage he knew the metal had softened and could be shaped.

After years of swinging his heavy hammer, his sweaty muscles were huge. Bending, twisting, he held the hot piece with a pair of tongs, pounding gold and bronze sections into a variety of resplendent and useful items. The metal might become a nail, sword, or even a goddess' canopy bed. The Greek god of the forge could create them all.

Usually Hephaestus worked on assignment, making items others had requested. A long list awaited his attention, but his current project took priority.

He was making a throne for his mother, Hera (HAYR-uh).[1] The royal seat he had designed would delight the queen of the gods, Hephaestus knew, as it was like no other in Olympus. Golden cuckoos and willow leaves decorated the back, a full moon hung above it, and white fur adorned the seat.

Hephaestus smiled grimly as he pictured Hera's pleased expression upon seeing the graceful throne. He had made it fancier than any of the other thrones on Mount Olympus. "When my mother sits on it," he chortled, "she will know how much I love her."

Hephaestus' reputation was well known. He had become skilled after spending years at his forge. Everyone knew he preferred working there than being with people.

His problems with people had started at birth. Unlike the other gods and goddesses who were born beautiful and perfectly formed, Hephaestus had entered the world with a humped back and skinny legs that stuck out from his torso like toothpicks. Black hair covered his body, and his swarthy face looked as pinched as a raisin.[2]

Hera was mortified at her baby's appearance. How could she, queen of the gods, have produced something so ugly? Hephaestus fussed constantly, annoying her further. Greatly aggravated, she put him and his crib in a closet in the back of her palace to keep from hearing his pitiful cries.

Hera couldn't escape the guffaws of ridicule from the other gods. "Hera has birthed the ugliest child in all Olympus!" they cried, until Hera wanted to plug her ears.

Hera strode furiously back and forth in her chambers. "First a babe that cries like a banshee and now a passel of gods who laugh at me!" she shrieked. Her face burned with shame. "That ugly son has brought nothing but trouble to me," she told herself. Her anger toward baby Hephaestus grew daily, even as she ignored him in the room where he stayed.

One day, Hephaestus cried so much that Hera's ears hurt. Her temper erupted. She stormed into Hephaestus' closet, picked him up, and threw him out the window. "Never again will the other gods laugh at me!" she cried.

Little Hephaestus fell from the top of Mount Olympus into the ocean. His splash attracted the attention of two sea nymphs, Thetis (THEE-tis) and Euronyme (yur-ON-ih-mee). They swam to his side and rescued him.

Thetis and Euronyme took Hephaestus to live with them in their underwater cave. For nine years he lived there happily. The nymphs took good care of him and loved him as their son. While he was in their grotto, he learned the art of blacksmithing.[3]

At first Hephaestus was content making simple items on the forge, like spoons and forks. Then he ventured into larger, more complex projects, such as furniture and buildings. Whenever he saw a metallic item around his home, he tried to create a stronger, more attractive piece.

Over the years Hephaestus spent many hours perfecting his skill, decorating the nymphs' grotto with graceful statues, gates, tables, and chairs made from metals and precious stones. People said he had the most talented hands in the world.[4]

He showed his appreciation to Thetis and Euronyme by making lovely cups, brooches, and other jewelry for them. A certain brooch with green, red, and blue gems was Thetis' favorite. She wore it everywhere, proud to show it to her friends. One day at a reception for the gods, Hera spied Thetis wearing the brooch. As the two began talking, Hera's eyes fastened on the pin. It sparkled around a delicate frame, and Hera's fingers itched to pin it to her own gown.

Hera asked Thetis where she had gotten the pin. At first the nymph refused to tell, but Hera persisted. With a resigned sigh, Thetis said, "Hephaestus, the babe you tossed from Mount Olympus many years ago, made the pin."

Hera was shocked. The son she thought was long gone had made the stunning item?

The next day Hera arrived at Thetis' grotto and knocked. When Hephaestus, standing with a stooped back and weak legs, opened the door, she greeted him with what she hoped looked like affection. "Oh, Hephaestus, my lost son! How I've missed you!" she cried, throwing her arms around his neck.

Hephaestus stood stiffly. After several minutes, he disengaged himself, then moved to shut the door in her face. She quickly inquired about his work.

"I've noticed Thetis wearing a gorgeous piece of jewelry. Where do you get ideas for your designs?"

Reluctantly, Hephaestus showed her the items he had made, not realizing that excitement crept into his voice as he talked about his work. But Hera noticed.

Thetis (left), who took care of Hephaestus as he grew up, was also the mother of the Greek warrior Achilles (right).

During the tour, Hera's mind churned madly. "If you can make gorgeous pieces with a single bellows," she said, "what could you do with twenty bellows?"[5]

Hephaestus hesitated. He had always yearned for a bigger forge on which to create larger projects like castles. But he didn't trust Hera.

For two days Hera tried to convince her son to return to Mount Olympus. "In the land of the gods you will have everything at your fingertips," she told him. "Ask, and it is yours."

Hephaestus refused her offer, but Hera would not give up. Finally, he rubbed his chin as if in thought. "I'll come to Olympus if you will answer one question."

"I'm the queen of the gods. What do you want to know?"

Hephaestus straightened until his face was close to hers. "Who is my father?"

The blood drained from Hera's face. "You have no father," she told him.

"Everyone has a father!" he cried. "I have a right to know mine!"

Hera silently turned away. Hephaestus glowered, then wiped his brow.

"Very well. I'll prepare a gift for you when I am ready to come to Olympus," he told her.

Hera's face lit with joy. She traveled back to Olympus, dreaming up plans for new furniture, statues, and jewelry made by Hephaestus. His question had disturbed her, but she put it out of her mind.

During the next several weeks, Hephaestus designed and built for his mother the finest golden throne ever seen on Olympus. When he had it delivered to her, she clapped her hands in delight. Then, before her maids and servants, she proudly sat on its plush seat.

As soon as she did, the arms of the chair locked around her, holding her fast. Hera struggled, but the strong bands around her body refused to loosen. "Release me!" she screamed.

Hera, queen of the gods, was Hephaestus' prisoner!

Hephaestus and Vulcan

Whenever the ancient Greeks discovered something helpful like fire, they said it must be the gift of a god. They then created stories, or myths, to explain the origins of the gift. They also attributed natural phenomena, such as volcanic activity, to the gods and their activities. Hephaestus, the Greek god of fire and metal-working, was believed to live in volcanoes. He was represented as a sturdy, muscular man with one leg shorter than

Temple of Hephaestus in Athens, Greece

the other, and with forging tools in his hand. He was worshiped at several locations, including Mount Lemnos, possibly because the area was volcanic and a jet of natural asphalt gas issued from its summit.

In Italy, the early Romans adopted the beliefs of the people they conquered, including those of the Greeks. They changed the Greek myths to fit Roman culture, and renamed the gods according to their language. Since the god of fire was thought to live in volcanoes, the Roman name for him became Vulcan.

The Romans thought Vulcan had his headquarters in a volcano on an island south of Italy called Sicily. There the god supposedly forged thunderbolts for Jupiter—the Roman equivalent of the Greeks' Zeus (ZOOS). Whenever a different mountain on the island began to belch fire and ash, the Romans believed the fire god had moved to a new home.

Vulcan was also associated with forges on the island of Lipari, the largest of a chain of seven volcanic islands called the Aeolians, about 27 miles (44 kilometers) from Sicily. These islands, which the Greeks associated with Aeolus, the god of the winds, extend from Mount Vesuvius to Mount Etna.

Besides the spewing of Lemnos, another jet burned steadily from Mount Moschylus in ancient Greece for centuries. Each of these mountains had a shrine that burned for Hephaestus.[6] Great festivals—the Hephaestia in Greece and the Vulcanalia in Rome—were celebrated in honor of him.[7]

French sculptor Guillame Coustou the Younger of France carved Hephaestus reclining on his forge in the late 1700s. The god leans on a newly made helmet.

HEPHAESTUS

CHAPTER 2

Another Fall

When Hephaestus heard that Hera was a captive in his specially made throne, he smiled with cold satisfaction. "My revenge for her callous attitude of not caring for me as a babe is now complete," he told Thetis and Euronyme. "I have imprisoned her so that everyone can view her humiliation. Perhaps now she will understand what it feels like to be forgotten and rejected."

All day and night, Hera tried to escape the throne's tenacious embrace—to no avail. The next morning she screamed at her husband, Zeus, for help.

Zeus, the king of the gods, ordered his strongest soldiers to tear the chair apart. The warriors struck the chair repeatedly with heavy swords, but it held. The other gods tried hacking through the bonds, but no one could loosen the chair's viselike grip.

"Find Hephaestus and order him to release me!" Hera demanded Zeus. "Now!"

Zeus quickly called for the messenger god, Hermes (HUR-meez). "Hephaestus must be brought to Olympus," he told the fleet-footed courier. "Tell him I command him to come at once and release Queen Hera." Immediately, Hermes flew off, his winged sandals fluttering in haste.

When Hermes relayed Zeus' words to Hephaestus, the god of fire refused to listen. "Hera has treated me badly and now she must pay," he said. Back on Olympus, Hermes delivered Hephaestus' message to Zeus.

Zeus called a meeting of the gods' council. "Hephaestus must be brought to Mount Olympus to free Hera," he said. "How can we get him here?"

After debating for several hours, the council decided to send Dionysus (dy-oh-NY-sus), the god of wine, to Hephaestus. They hoped he and his wine could persuade Hephaestus to free Hera.

Dionysus took some of his best wine to Hephaestus' workshop. "Here, my friend," he said, "take a sip." He held out a goblet filled with a red velvety liquid. The heady scent of freshly picked grapes wafted to Hephaestus' nostrils.

Standing over a hot forge did make Hephaestus thirsty. He welcomed the drink—and the many others that followed. Soon Hephaestus swayed on his feet. Without protest, he allowed Dionysus to lead him to Olympus and Hera, who was still wriggling in the prison of her chair.[1]

Hephaestus raised his arms as though to release Hera. Then he stopped. "I asked you once who my father was," he reminded her. "You denied me an answer. Tell me now who my sire is if you wish to be released."

Hera and Zeus had three children: Ares, the god of war; Eileithyia, the goddess of childbirth; and Hebe, the goddess of youth. Hephaestus may have been their fourth child, but some myths claim he was Hera's alone.

Hera spoke slowly, as though to a young child. "You . . . have . . . no . . . father."

Hephaestus shook his shaggy head in protest. "Everyone has a father," he cried. "I must have one. Swear by the River Styx that what you say is true."[2] Swearing by the Styx, the river that separated the living from the dead, was the greatest oath the gods could take.

"What I have told you is true." Hera sighed. "Before you were born, Zeus paid more attention to Artemis, his daughter with Leto, than to his children with me. This made me jealous. When Zeus gave Artemis gifts like a bow and quiver, sixty nymphs, all the mountains in the world, and a city, I swore my next child would not have a father. You are the result of that decision."

Hephaestus stared at Hera for several moments. Then, silently, he released her.[3] (Another myth says Zeus was Hephaestus' father.[4])

The relationship between Hephaestus and Hera improved. He accepted her offer to move to Olympus to work in her forge. She provided twenty bellows for him, and though she had a long list of items for him to make, she patiently allowed him to create items of his choice. Eventually, he made lovely works of art for her, which pleased them both.

Soon the land of the gods looked like a new place. Before Hephaestus arrived, Mount Olympus had been drab and plain. But with his artistic touches it became a fantastic palace, filled with golden tables, chairs, chalices, and torch stands. For each god, Hephaestus made a magnificent bed.[5] Zeus and Hera's was the grandest of all.

After Hephaestus and Hera reconciled, Hephaestus became fond of Hera. On one occasion he even saved her from destruction. Zeus and Hera fought constantly. One day Zeus discovered she had led a conspiracy against him. Furious, he hung her upside down from the sky with an anvil fastened to her wrists. Though troubled by the display, the other deities lacked the courage to attempt to rescue her.

Hephaestus had no such inhibition. When he saw his mother hanging in that precarious position, he rushed to Zeus, demanding the king of the gods to release her.

It was a gallant gesture, but some thought Hephaestus would have been wiser to stay out of the fight. Zeus, fuming, glared at Hephaestus.

"How dare you tell the king of the gods what to do!" Then he picked Hephaestus up and threw him out the window.

It must have seemed like a nightmare to Hephaestus to fall from Mount Olympus a second time. For an entire day he felt the cold rush of wind against his body as he fell and fell and fell. When he finally landed, the wind was knocked out of him. Barely breathing, he lay still for a long time, hoping the pain he felt everywhere would go away. At one point he tried to move his legs but could not. He figured he had broken them, and he groaned in frustration.

The warmth and brightness of the sun convinced him he hadn't fallen all the way to the underworld. A tantalizing scent hung in the air, and he realized he had fallen in the midst of a vineyard. But where was he?

In his *Finding of Vulcan on Lemnos,* Italian painter Piero di Cosimo shows a band of nymphs helping Hephaestus to his feet after his second fall from Olympus.

Hephaestus slowly opened one eye and lifted his head. Dizziness overcame him and his head fell back. Several minutes later, he tried again. This time his vision cleared and Hephaestus heard voices.

A small face popped out from between two rows of grapes. Upon spying Hephaestus lying a few feet away, the child looked first surprised, then frightened. "Papa! Come look!"

Hephaestus let his head fall back to the ground, unable to determine his whereabouts and not caring. The next time he opened his eyes, he was lying on a soft bed inside what seemed to be a cottage. The roaring fire a few feet away warmed him, and he relaxed and slept again.

The volcanic island of Lemnos offered Hephaestus a place to heal physically and mentally from his experiences in Olympus.

The next time he awoke, he sat up, though he still couldn't move his legs. He saw a man and the child from the vineyard watching him.

"Where am I?" Hephaestus asked.

"The island of Lemnos," the man replied.

The people gave Hephaestus food and drink and treated his injured legs. The man told Hephaestus the damage to his legs was permanent. "You will always walk with a limp," he said solemnly. But when he presented Hephaestus with a sturdy, elegant walking stick, made by the people of Lemnos, the fire god accepted the news with equanimity. He could do nothing about it, so he made the best of it.

Hephaestus stayed in Lemnos, where the people helped him learn how to walk again. They laughed constantly—though not in ridicule—and Hephaestus felt happy. Their exuberance helped him forget the pain in his legs and in his heart.

Eventually Zeus pardoned Hephaestus and invited him back to Olympus. Instead, Hephaestus set up a forge in a volcano on the island and taught the inhabitants metalworking. Two tosses out the window were enough to convince Hephaestus it was safer to stay away from the Greek gods' abode.[6]

With all the sad events that occurred in his life, Hephaestus could be viewed as a victim. But this great god refused to give up on life completely. Away from Olympus, he created a new life with people who appreciated him.

Some people believe that the Greeks imparted a limp on Hephaestus because in primitive times, blacksmiths were considered valuable. They were purposely lamed to prevent them from running off and joining enemy tribes.[7]

Even with a limp, Hephaestus persevered, looking for the good that life had to offer.

Hephaestus in Literature

The Greek myth about Hephaestus' fall from Mount Olympus is told in several pieces of ancient literature. The poet John Milton refers to a fall by Hephaestus in Book I of *Paradise Lost* (1.742-6):

Hephaestus

> . . . From morn
> To noon he fell, from noon to dewy eve,
> A summer's day; and with the setting sun
> Dropped from the zenith, like a falling star,
> On Lemnos, the Ægean isle.

In his hymn to Hephaestus, Homer sets a scene in which Hera tells the gods how Hephaestus came to be rescued after she threw him out the window: "But my son Hephaistos . . . shrivelled of foot, a shame and a disgrace to me in heaven I myself took in my hands and cast out so that he fell in the great sea. But silver-shod Thetis the daughter of Nereus took and cared for him with her sisters."[8]

Homer again writes about Hephaestus' death-defying fall in the *Iliad,* as Hephaestus addresses his mother Hera, "There was a time once before now I was minded to help you, and he [Zeus] caught me by the foot and threw me from the magic threshold, and all day long I dropped helpless, and about sunset I landed in Lemnos, and there was not much life left in me."[9]

In *The Library,* which has been attributed to Apollodorus, we read of this interpretation of the argument that stirred Zeus' anger against Hephaestus: "Zeus threw him [Hephaistos] from the sky for helping Hera when she was in chains. Zeus had hung her from Olympos as punishment for setting a storm on Herakles as he was sailing back from his conquest of Troy. Hephaistos landed on Lemnos, crippled in both legs, but saved by Thetis."[10]

Apparently, the Greek philosopher Plato didn't think much of the story: "But Hera's fetterings by her son and the hurling out of heaven of Hephaistos by his father [Zeus] when he was trying to save his mother from a beating, and the battles of the gods in Homer's verse are things that we must not admit into our city either wrought in allegory or without allegory. For the young are not able to distinguish what is and what is not allegory."[11]

In an ancient Greek vase painting, Hephaestus raises Pandora from the earth.

HEPHAESTUS

CHAPTER 3

Pandora

Zeus slammed his fist against the table. "How dare he!" he shouted. "How dare Prometheus [proh-MEE-thee-us] steal the gift of fire from me and offer it to mankind! Prometheus must pay!"

Prometheus, a Titan, had helped Zeus overthrow Zeus' father, Cronos (KROH-nus), in the war between the Titans and the Greek gods. After the battle, Zeus ruled the gods and earth; his brother Poseidon (poh-SY-dun) ruled the seas; and another brother, Hades (HAY-deez), ruled the Underworld, the land of the dead. Later, Prometheus rebelled against Zeus because he was hostile toward mankind.

Prometheus was a master of many skills. According to one tradition of Apollodorus, he made the first men out of clay.[1] (Greek mythology states the only mortal race on earth at that time was male.) Prometheus instructed them in various arts, including architecture, astronomy, navigation, and medicine. He was kind toward humans and even offered them protection when he could.

In contrast, Zeus had a stern attitude toward mankind and harassed them. Hostility between the two gods broke out when Prometheus returned the gift of fire to men, which Zeus had taken away. Zeus was so angry with Prometheus that he decided to punish the mortal men. He asked Hephaestus to make a woman.

Hephaestus sculpted a woman from clay according to Zeus' specifications. The creature's form became that of a shy, modest maiden, while her face resembled that of an ethereal goddess. Then Hephaestus allowed the other gods and goddesses to add to his creation.

Athena (uh-THEE-nuh), the goddess of wisdom, dressed the woman in white, veiled her face, and decorated her with jewels. Aphrodite (af-roh-DY-tee), the goddess of love, anointed her with grace and charm. Hermes gave her an appealing voice filled with lies, flattery, seduction, treachery, and shamelessness. The Four Winds breathed life into her.[2]

As a final touch, Hephaestus forged a golden crown and placed it on the woman's head. Zeus called the creation Pandora (pan-DOR-uh). Her name, which means "all gifts," reflects the adornment of gifts from the gods upon her birth.[3]

Before setting her on earth, Zeus handed Pandora a gorgeous box (or jar) decorated with gold filigree and exquisite drawings. "You may enjoy looking at this, Pandora, but do not look inside," he said. He chuckled when she left with her gift, because he knew she would not be able to obey.

At first Pandora had no problem with the command. She stayed busy and happy on earth, getting to know her new environment. As the first woman, she had plenty of admirers.

One man caught her attention. Epimetheus (eh-pih-MEE-thee-us) was honest and hardworking, and he adored Pandora. The two fell in love.

Prometheus, Epimetheus' older brother, warned Epimetheus not to marry Pandora. "Her dowry will unleash evil into the world!" he said. He was referring to the box Zeus had given her.

"You don't know her!" Epimetheus protested. "Pandora would not hurt anyone."

"Don't question me. Just obey!" his brother demanded.

Epimetheus loved Pandora and refused to believe she could be so foolish as to open the box given to her by Zeus.

One version of the myth says Prometheus knew the

contents of the jar because he had filled it with the world's woes. Another myth said he knew because he could see into the future. The name Prometheus means "forethought." In contrast, *Epimetheus* means "afterthought."[4]

Epimetheus disregarded his brother's advice and married Pandora. When he accepted the container as her dowry, he recalled Prometheus' words and warned Pandora, "Do not open that box, my love. It may hold curses."

At first Pandora heeded Epimetheus' advice. However, after the wedding, her curiosity could wait no longer. Alone for a few minutes in her chamber, she picked up the intricate box. "Surely a quick peek will not hurt anything," she thought. Lifting the lid, she peered into its dark interior.

A stench greeted her nostrils, and a swarm of nasty winged beings flew into her face. Startled, Pandora threw the box on the floor, covering her face and eyes and backing away from it. For several seconds she sat staring at it, frozen in fright. Then she scrambled to the container, hurrying to replace the cover. She didn't know what was inside, but she knew it was evil.

Too late! Zeus had filled the box with all the evils that could beset the world—Old Age, Sorrow, Illness, Plague, and Famine. These had escaped, but all was not lost. By the time Pandora shut the lid, one spirit remained inside—Hope. By shutting the lid, Pandora captured the one spirit that enabled humankind to go on living, despite adversity.[5]

In modern English, the expression *Pandora's box* has come to mean a gift that at first seems valuable but turns out to be a source of troubles.

Zeus also punished Prometheus by shackling him to a rock. He cursed Prometheus with a monstrous eagle that every day ate the Titan's liver. Every night, the liver grew back. Hephaestus made the chains that bound him, and only the hero Hercules (HER-kyoo-leez), a son of Zeus, could free him from his torment.[6]

Between Hera and Pandora, Hephaestus' associations with women had been sorrow-filled. The worst was yet to come.

Day after day, he worked in his forge in Lemnos, twisting and turning the pieces of near-white metal, pounding them with his hammer into smooth objects of beauty. One piece of which he was especially proud was an armlet studded with emeralds and rubies. He shaped the jeweled piece, then peered at it closely, studying it for imperfections. A few more gentle taps, then he nodded. "This armlet will make a fine gift for a goddess," he said to the giant Cyclopes (SY-kloh-peez) standing around him.

These one-eyed monsters helped Hephaestus manufacture cunning and useful objects from metals found in the depths of the earth. Other helpers at his side were golden handmaidens, whom he had also forged.

Though Hephaestus refused to return to Olympus, he kept his crew busy, building many complex items for the gods there. He constructed magnificent golden palaces for each of the Olympic gods, and their furniture as well, using precious stones from the earth's interior. He also crafted much of the other magnificent equipment of the gods, including frightening thunderbolts for Zeus, Hermes' helmet and sandals, and the bow and arrows of Eros (AYR-ohs), the god of love.[7]

Each time he formed darts for Eros, Hephaestus thought again of his desire to marry. He was convinced that with his looks, no goddess would want him.

As he held up the beautiful armlet, his shoulders sagged. Carefully setting the piece on his anvil, he removed his tunic and left the forge. The Cyclopes knew better than to follow. Head hanging low, Hephaestus walked along the beach, wishing for the thousandth time he had a wife for whom he could create beautiful jewelry.

Over the years, Hephaestus had developed strong arms and shoulders from swinging the heavy hammer at the forge. But he still could not straighten his back. His legs were too shattered. "If the gods could see me now, they would never stop laughing," he muttered.

The thought kept him from attending parties and meetings on Olympus, but it didn't keep him from falling in love. He first wooed Athena, whom he had known since she was born. In fact, Hephaestus had a hand in her birth.

One day, Zeus was suffering from a terrible headache. He summoned all the gods to Olympus to help him find a cure. Their efforts were in vain. Unable to endure the racking pain any longer, Zeus begged Hephaestus to cut open his head with an ax. No sooner was the operation performed

An ancient Greek vase painting shows Athena leaping from the head of Zeus. Hephaestus, who helped with the birth, would try to persuade the goddess to marry him.

than Athena sprang from her father's head. She was fully grown and clad in glittering armor, holding a spear, and chanting a triumphant song of victory.[8]

Hephaestus and Athena became the two patrons of handicrafts. Athena knew more than anyone about pottery, weaving, and the useful arts. She taught him how to handle tools.[9] He protected smiths, while she protected weavers.[10] They shared temples at Athens.[11] On the Agora, the public square in Athens, the temple to Hephaestus was near the Parthenon, Athena's temple.

Many gods wanted to marry the magnificent Athena, including Hephaestus. But Athena didn't want a husband. Hephaestus thought he'd try to change her mind.

During the Trojan War—the great conflict between Greece and Troy—Athena asked Hephaestus to make her a set of weapons. "I don't want to borrow Zeus' armor during this critical time," she explained. "I'd prefer to have my own." Hephaestus agreed.

Athena ducked into Hephaestus' forge to watch him make her armor.

When it was completed, he held out his arms to her, hoping for a kiss. Normally, Hephaestus didn't seek affection. But he mistakenly thought Athena would reward him with love. Startled at Hephaestus' action, Athena pushed him away and ran from the forge. Although they did not embrace, a child was born from this meeting. His name was Erichthonius (ayr-ik-THOH-nee-us), which means "earth," because the earth, not Athena, carried this baby to term.[12]

After Athena's rejection, Hephaestus no longer believed in love or marriage. He returned to his forge, sad and lonely. He didn't know it, but a bride was in his future. The question was, would she bring him happiness?

The Italian-born sixteenth-century painter Paris Bordone created the painful scene of Athena rejecting Hephaestus' advances.

The Greek Eve

The tale of Pandora, found in the writings of Hesiod, a Greek poet, bears a resemblance to the story of Eve and the Garden of Eden in the Bible. Both stories attempt to explain the origin of women.

In each story, man was created before woman. According to the Bible, the divine Potter, Yahweh (God), shaped clay and gave it life by blowing breath into its nostrils. The first man, Adam, was thus created from the earth.

Pandora had no idea what power—and evils—lay within the box Zeus had given her as a dowry for her marriage to Epimetheus.

In another biblical account, God provided Adam with a garden to till and enjoy. Realizing that solitary life and work was lonely, God formed other animal species for human companionship. Then God created the first woman, Eve, from Adam's rib.

Adam loved Eve as his wife, and God told the couple they could have anything in the garden, but they were not to eat from the Tree of Life because it would make them die. A serpent, seen as Satan, came into the garden and suggested that the command from God to Adam and Eve was not true. "Ye shall not surely die," the serpent told them. Instead, he said, "your eyes shall be opened, and ye shall be as gods, knowing good and evil." Eve "took of the fruit thereof, and did eat, and gave also unto her husband with her; and he did eat." (Genesis, 3.1–6)

Afterward, God punished the couple by sending them from the Garden of Eden. He sentenced Adam to a life of hard labor working with the soil. Eve was given pain in childbirth. After they left the garden, they settled down and began a family.

Hesiod formed a cynical synopsis of the creation story of woman: "Any man who trusts a woman trusts a deceiver."[13]

In his 1732 painting *Venus at Vulcan's Forge*, François Boucher portrayed the wife of Vulcan as discontented. Just as the Romans called Hephaestus Vulcan, their name for Aphrodite was Venus.

HEPHAESTUS

CHAPTER 4

A Wedding but No Marriage

Hera knew Hephaestus desired a wife, so she arranged for him to marry Aphrodite, the goddess of love. There is no single myth that explains the origin of Aphrodite. Some myths say she sprang from the foam of the sea, since *aphros* means "foam" in Greek.[1] Another myth claimed she was the daughter of Zeus and the Oceanic Titan Dione.[2] No matter what her origin, Aphrodite appeared as a beautiful goddess, fully formed from the day she was born.

As might be expected, when Hephaestus heard he was to marry the goddess of love, he was thrilled. "I will be the happiest god alive!" he shouted. Unfortunately, Aphrodite did not share his excitement over the arrangement.

With her beauty, Aphrodite beguiled every god on Olympus and man on earth. Over time, her beauty became an evil tool she used to destroy men. She smiled sweetly at their attempts to please her, but the minute their backs were turned, she mocked them.

The wedding of Aphrodite and Hephaestus took place on Olympus. Hephaestus thanked Zeus by giving him several finely made items from his forge. As a wedding present, he gave Aphrodite a magic girdle he had made. That may not have been the wisest gift, because each time she wore it, men fell in love with her. Hephaestus wanted her to wear the girdle just for him, but she wore it on trips to the market, temple, everywhere. With the girdle, she felt important and powerful. "It's a disgrace to be the wife of a sooty-faced blacksmith who limps and walks with a stoop," she told the nymphs who tended her.

After their wedding, Aphrodite tried for a short time to live with Hephaestus in his castle on Mount Etna. But the gloomy atmosphere made her feel depressed and unsure. "How can I bewitch men when I am stuck in this cave?" she asked herself.

It wasn't long before Aphrodite began looking for happiness outside her home. She found it in the arms of Ares (AYR-eez), the god of war. He was fair-skinned, straight-limbed, impetuous, drunken, and quarrelsome. He had no manners and no education, and he loved to fight.

In the *Iliad,* a Greek epic poem that described the siege of Troy, the poet Homer calls Ares murderous, bloodstained, and a coward who bellowed with pain and ran away when wounded. (Some myths say Ares was the son of Zeus and Hera, making him Hephaestus' brother.) Aphrodite thought he was wonderful.

She kept her relationship with Ares a secret from Hephaestus. However, one night the sun god Helios (HEE-lee-ohs) saw Ares and Aphrodite

Jacques-Louis David, in *Mars Disarmed by Venus and the Three Graces,* shows Ares, portrayed in Roman mythology as Mars, with Venus. The clumsiness of the Three Graces conveys the wickedness of this relationship.

In *The Forge of Vulcan,* painted by Diego Velázquez in 1630, the sun-god Apollo (left), not Helios, has come to tell Hephaestus (facing the viewer) about his wife and Ares. The other workers there are the Cyclopes, though Velázquez painted them with two eyes.

kissing behind a pillar at the palace. Helios immediately flew to Hephaestus to tell him about it.

Hephaestus sucked in his breath when he heard the news. Aphrodite had found love with another! The smith god's heart split in two. Yet when he asked Zeus to intervene, the king of the gods only laughed.

"What did you expect?" he said. "You gave your wife a girdle that makes her irresistible! Can you blame your brother if he falls in love with her when she wears it?"

Hephaestus shuffled back to his smithy, angry and sick at heart, his crooked legs nearly crumpling in despair. He dealt with his pain the only way he knew how—by working in his forge. He set his great anvil on the block, hoping to design a new thunderbolt for Zeus. Suddenly, a thought came to him.

Vulcan forging weapons is one of the many images in the fresco *Allegory of the Divine Providence and Barberini Power*, painted by Pietro da Cortona in the 1630s. The image of Vulcan symbolizes the importance of being prepared for war.

Hephaestus knew he was as clever as Ares was strong. He also knew he could create strong weapons and equally lovely metallic pieces, such as the world had never seen.

Hephaestus asked the Cyclopes and the golden handmaidens to leave so that he could work alone, then he pumped the bellows until a huge fire crackled. For the next several weeks he worked in his chamber. Hard hammering could be heard coming from the forge deep into the night. When Hephaestus finally emerged, he carried not a suit of armor nor a palace gate, but a bronze hunting net as fine as silk.

When the people of Lemnos saw it, they asked for whom he had forged the elegant item. Hephaestus smiled. "It is a gift," he said, though he refused to announce the recipient.

The villagers said to one another, "It must be for the goddess Aphrodite, whom Hephaestus holds in such high esteem."

One day soon after, Aphrodite left for Cyprus, her favorite island. Hephaestus watched her go, then entered the castle, intent on his mission. He picked up the gossamer net and attached it to the corners of his home. The net was stronger than it looked, nearly unbreakable and barely visible. It hung like a thinly spun web of a spider.

When Aphrodite returned from Cyprus several days later, she looked more beautiful than ever. Her helpers, the Graces, had bathed her and rubbed oil of ambrosia into her flawless skin. Hephaestus smiled and said, "I must leave you for a while, my dear. My business should allow me to return in a few days."

Aphrodite waved him off. She did not offer to go with him.

As soon as Hephaestus left, Aphrodite sent for Ares, and he hurried to the castle. Inside, the two tried to embrace, but instead found themselves tangled in Hephaestus' net with its unyielding chains.

The couple wriggled, trying to shed themselves of the web, but the links clung tightly. Ares and Aphrodite hollered for help.

Hiding around the corner of his castle, Hephaestus heard their pleas and smiled. He had snuck to a side window, where he could see Aphrodite and Ares thrashing under the netting. Then he called the rest of the Olympic gods to his home.

"My wife has dishonored me," he grimly told them, pointing to the ensnared couple. Ares and Aphrodite paused inside their glossy prison to glare at him and the other gods. "I will not release Aphrodite," said Hephaestus, "until the valuable gifts I gave to her father, Zeus, at our wedding are restored to me."

Dutch painter Martin Van Heemskerk shows the fine netting trapping Venus and Mars, and the gods looking on with no sympathy for Vulcan.

Zeus turned away from Hephaestus and said, "I will not return the gifts. She is your wife. Leave me out of your problems."

The other gods didn't sympathize with Hephaestus either. "We wish our wives were as beautiful as Aphrodite," they said.

Poseidon sensed Hephaestus' dismay. "Since Zeus refuses to pay, I'll see that Ares pays for the marital gifts if you release him and Aphrodite," he said.

"What if he refuses?"

"I'll pay myself."

Hephaestus gloomily agreed. As soon as the gossamer chains dropped, Ares fled to Thrace, where a war was raging. Aphrodite scurried back to Cyprus.

Neither Ares nor Poseidon paid Hephaestus for the wedding gifts. Worse, Hephaestus allowed Aphrodite back into his castle, where she continued to attract the attention of other gods.[3]

Hephaestus was intelligent enough to create beautiful works of art, even beings such as Pandora and his handmaidens to assist him, but he could not understand his wife. That seems to have been the lament of men in every culture since the world began. Perhaps the mythmakers who developed this story about Hephaestus were in similar situations.

Poseidon

A Helpful God

Many of the Greek gods performed miraculous feats, such as Hermes flying back and forth between Olympus and Hades, and Demeter, who caused plants around the world to grow or die, depending on her mood. In contrast, Hephaestus spent his time performing an amazingly mundane, humanlike job—standing over a hot forge, creating works of art that would enhance the lives of others. In nearly every story created about him, he was at his volcanic forge, content to work alone, though often for deeds of gallantry that others would be exalted for, such as Achilles.

In the *Iliad,* Homer lists the intricate process Hephaestus performed in designing Achilles' shield:

Hephaestus . . . went to his bellows,
Turned them toward the fire, and ordered them to work.
And the bellows, all twenty, blew on the crucibles,
Blasting out waves of heat . . .
He cast durable bronze onto the fire, and tin,
Precious gold and silver. Then he positioned
His enormous anvil up on its block
And grasped his mighty hammer
In one hand, and in the other his tongs.
He made a shield first, heavy and huge,
Every inch of it intricately designed.
He threw a triple rim around it, glittering
Like lightning, and he made the strap silver.
The shield itself was five layers thick, and he
Crafted its surface with all of his genius.
On it he made the earth, the sky, the sea,
The unwearied sun, and the moon near full,
And all the signs that garland the sky, . . .
On it he made two cities, peopled
And beautiful.[4]

For his trouble and dedication, Hephaestus, like many of the Greek gods, was worshiped by followers. Besides the Hephaestia and the Vulcanalia, the god of fire was celebrated, along with Athena, at a festival called Chalceia in Attica. He was also connected with the religious group called the *Hephaistoi* (the Hephaestus-men) in Lemnos. Those who followed this religion claimed their founders had been children of the blacksmith god.[5]

35

In 1803, Johann Heinrich Füssli painted the touching reunion between
Thetis and Hephaestus as Thetis requests new armor for her son, Achilles.
The golden handmaidens of Hephaestus cling to the god.

HEPHAESTUS

CHAPTER 5

Armor for Achilles

All the gods, including Hephaestus, were involved in the Trojan War—the war the Greeks declared in order to win Helen, Agamemnon's queen, back from Paris, the prince of Troy. Besides his feats on the battlefield, Hephaestus forged armor and weapons for the combatants.

Thetis scurried toward the bronze palace gates of Hephaestus' castle, her breath coming in shallow puffs. Her heart pounded as she pushed against the heavy barriers. Pausing to take a quick gulp of air, she continued, hastily slipping around the gates before climbing the steps to the castle's great doors. She hammered on them, hoping someone would answer.

After what seemed an eternity, a goddess Thetis didn't recognize answered her knock. The gray-haired sea nymph nearly fell into the stranger's arms in relief.

"Please," begged Thetis, weeping, "I must see Hephaestus! He is the only one who can save my son's life!"[1]

After his disastrous relationship with Aphrodite, Hephaestus had married Charis (KAR-is), whose name means "Grace." The two lived quietly in Hephaestus' castle, Charis tending to household duties while Hephaestus worked in his forge.

Now Charis studied Thetis' anxious face with concern. She slipped an arm around the visitor, ushering her to an ornate silver chair Hephaestus had made. "Please rest while I tell my husband you wish to see him," she said, patting Thetis' hand. "I know Hephaestus will want to help his adopted mother, of whom he always speaks with love and respect. Calm yourself, my lady, I beg you." Her gentle voice soothed Thetis, and she relaxed in her chair as Charis hurried to the forge.

Charis found Hephaestus, as usual, sweating before his mighty bellows. When she explained their visitor's presence and purpose, the sooty god immediately doused the fire, locked up his implements, and, with a sponge, wiped his hands, face, neck, and shaggy chest. Then, putting on his best tunic, he turned to Charis. "Take me to her," he said.

Hephaestus limped behind Charis to the drawing room. When he saw Thetis, his homely face lit up. "How wonderful that the noblest nymph has visited me," he said, covering Thetis' hand with his two large calloused ones. "You who once saved me from peril are always welcome here."

Charis had heard Hephaestus tell the story of how Hera had tossed him from Mount Olympus into the sea, and how Thetis and Euronyme had rescued him. She knew Hephaestus was thankful to Thetis for raising him and would not begrudge Thetis any request.

"You must help me!" Thetis cried, tightening her grip on Hephaestus' hand.

"What can I do for you?" he asked gently.

"My son Achilles is on the shores of Troy, waiting to join the battle against Paris. He had refused to fight in order to annoy his commander, Agamemnon, but then his friend Patroclus fought instead in Achilles' armor. Now Patroclus has been slain by the mighty Trojan prince Hector, who robbed the dear corpse of Achilles' armor. With the death of Patroclus, Achilles turned his anger from Agamemnon to Hector and the Trojans, and now he's ready to lead his men into battle. But he has no armor. Will you make him a helmet and shield, a cuirass, and greaves fitted with ankle pieces as protection?"

Achilles

Hephaestus smiled. "Be of good courage, my beloved mother," he said. "I will save your son from the power of death by making his armor so strong and splendid he will rejoice and it will dazzle the eyes of every mortal who beholds it!"

Thetis smiled in relief, and Hephaestus headed for his forge, where he again fired up his bellows and began to work. He chose bronze, silver, and gold to put in the melting-vats. Using the bellows to blow hot air to make them pliable, he then selected the strongest pieces, setting them on his great anvil and shaping them with well-laid blows of his mighty hammer.

Hephaestus began with the shield. He chose the purest silver to form the straps. He created intricate designs on the outer surface of the shield, etching designs of the earth, sea, and heaven with the sun, moon, and constellations. He added two cities to the design, one happy with bridal rites and torch-lit feasts with an assembly of the people, and the other showing a city at war. Within the walls were women, young children, and old men, while outside, warriors lay in ambush. On another part of the shield was a scene of the tumult of battle with wounded men and the fight for bodies and armor. Hephaestus also sketched a field with loosened clods and plows and oxen. He hoped all these scenes would give Achilles courage and skill in battle.

Replica of Achilles' shield

When Hephaestus had finished the shield, he forged a breastplate brighter and stronger than any in the world. Next came a massive helmet that was topped with a crest of gold. Last, he created greaves of beaten tin for Achilles' legs. By working all night, he could give the finished items to Thetis just as the sun was peeking over the horizon.

"I am honored to help the woman who treated me as a beloved son," he said to her, his voice husky with emotion.

In his painting *Thetis Bringing the Armor to Achilles II*, Benjamin West captures Achilles just before his sadness over the loss of Patroclus turns to rage for battle.

Thetis seized the armor as though she were a hawk diving to pluck its prey from the ground. She turned to go, then whirled and hugged Hephaestus tightly, giving him a grateful smile. As she carried away the impressive pieces, hope for her son's survival filled her heart.

Upon entering the valley where Achilles waited with his troops, Thetis saw her son standing guard over the body of Patroclus. She laid Hephaestus' magnificent set of armor before him, and her son's eyes flashed.[2] Achilles' loud cry mustered his soldiers, who trembled at the armor's fearsome sight.

About his ankles, Achilles fastened the greaves. Around his chest he fastened the silver-studded breastplate, while over his shoulders he slung his great sword of tempered bronze. When he raised the stately helmet and set it on his head, the golden plume shimmered, catching the first rays of the morning sun. The head of Achilles glowed as if he were anointed with divine fire.

Achilles told his soldiers, "Watch over the body of my fallen comrade, Patroclus. When the battle is won, I will return to give him a proper burial." Then he took up his new shield and grabbed his spear, ready at last for battle.

As Achilles slew more and more Trojans, their bodies began to block the River Scamander. In a rage, Scamander tried to drown Achilles.[3] Hera, who favored the Greeks, did not want Achilles to die. She asked Hephaestus for help. According to the *Iliad*,

> Hephaestus launched his grim inhuman blaze.
> First he shot into flames and burned the plain,
> ignited hordes of corpses, squads Achilles slaughtered—
> he scorched the whole plain and the shining river shrank. . . .
> [Scamander] screamed in flames, his clear currents bubbling up
> like a cauldron whipped by crackling fire as it melts down
> the lard of a fat swine . . .
>   He stopped—overwhelmed
> by the torrid blast of the Master Craftsman god of fire—"[4]

Thus Hephaestus nearly dried up the furious river.

In the sculpture by Herman Wilhelm Bissen, Hephaestus is shown as less brutish than the myths describe him.

Near the end of the Trojan War, the great Achilles died. Thetis brought a golden urn, fashioned by Hephaestus, for the hero's ashes. The remains of Achilles were mixed with those of his friend Patroclus.[5]

Hephaestus influenced many important Greek myths and mythology, bringing pathos (emotion), humor, and appreciation for art to Greek society. He was a pioneer god in many ways. He was the first "unattractive" god, through no fault of his own. He was the first god, according to some myths, to have no father. He was also the first god to have a physical handicap.

Even though the story of Hephaestus was written thousands of years ago, we can see parallels from his life in our own lives. Most of us would like to change at least one part of our bodies. In addition, we all have at least one family member we would like to alter.

Hephaestus had many sad and discouraging events take place in his life. He was rejected by his mother, yet he chose to live amicably with the people of Lemnos. He was rejected by his wife, yet he did not give up on love. His physical disability could have hindered him from doing many godlike functions, but he didn't let it stop him. He became respected for his blacksmithing talents and for his willingness to share them with others.

The myths about Hephaestus focus on his choice to spend his time creating new works that brought joy and power to others. He chose to serve through his sorrow and pain, and found satisfaction in doing so. We would do well to follow Hephaestus' example.

Vulcan, the Roman god of the forge, helped Aeneas, a Trojan warrior, in much the same way as Hephaestus helped Achilles. When Aeneas, the legendary founder of the Roman race, arrived in Italy to do battle, his mother, Venus, fretted over his lack of armor. Venus asked Vulcan, who was her husband, to make

Venus Ordering Arms from Vulcan for Aeneas,
Jean Restout II

Aeneas new weapons and armor that would aid him in battle. Vulcan agreed. He commanded his workers, the Cyclopes, to begin forging Aeneas' special armor inside the great volcano Mount Etna.

One night, after his Roman army had marched all day and were preparing to fight the next, Aeneas was shocked to see his mother appear in his camp. She presented him with the armor that Vulcan had completed—helmet, corslet, sword, spear, and shield. The items were exceedingly strong and well crafted. Aeneas went on to use his armor in battle.

Aeneas is best known from Virgil's *Aeneid,* but he was also a part of early Greek mythology as the son of Aphrodite and the Trojan prince Anchises. In the *Iliad,* he is second in importance only to the Trojan leader Hector, whereas Achilles was the greatest of the Greek leaders who fought at Troy. When Achilles and Aeneas met on the battlefield, Poseidon had to step in to keep them from killing each other.[6]

Aeneas' shield, like Achilles', showed scenes from everyday life, the cosmos, and the world of the gods. Virgil also chose to have Vulcan forge the future of Rome on the shield of Aeneas, scenes "of events beyond/his scope of knowledge." When he lifted the shield, he "hoisted to his shoulder/the destinies and the fame of his descendants."[7]

Chapter 1. The First Fall

1. Robert Graves, *Greek Gods and Heroes* (New York: Dell Publishing, 1960), p.15.

2. Donald Richardson, *Great Zeus and All His Children* (Englewood Cliffs, NJ: Prentice-Hall, Inc., 1984), p. 15

3. Jenny March, *Cassell's Dictionary of Classical Mythology* (NY: Sterling Publishing Company, Inc.), p. 370.

4. Richardson, p. 15.

5. Ibid., p. 16.

6. H.A. Guerber, *The Myths of Greece and Rome* (New York: London House & Maxwell, 1963), p. 85.

7. Guerber, p. 87.

Chapter 2. Another Fall

1. H.A. Guerber, *The Myths of Greece and Rome* (New York: London House & Maxwell, 1963), p. 85.

2. Robert Graves, *The Greek Myths,* Vol.1 (New York: Penguin Books, 1955), p. 51.

3. Hesiod, *Theogony,* trans. Dorothea Wender (NY: Penguin Books, 1973), lines 924 ff.

4. Apollodorus, *The Library,* trans. Sir James George Frazer (Cambridge, MA: Harvard University Press; London: William Heinemann Ltd., 1921), 1.3.5.

5. Donald Richardson, *Great Zeus and All His Children* (Englewood Cliffs, NJ: Prentice-Hall, Inc., 1984), p. 15.

6. Guerber, p. 85.

7. Graves, *The Greek Myths,* p. 88.

8. *Homeric Hymn 3 to Pythian Apollo,* edited by Hugh G. Evelyn-White, line 310, http://www.perseus.tufts.edu/hopper/text?doc=Perseus%3Atext%3A1999.01.0138%3Ahymn%3D3

9. Homer, *Iliad,* translated by Robert Fagles (New York: Penguin Putnam, 1990), Book 18, line 136.

10. Apollodorus, 1.19.

11. Plato, *Republic,* per Stories of Hephaestus, *Theoi,* http://www.theoi.com/Olympios/HephaistosMyths.html

Chapter 3. Pandora

1. Apollodorus, *The Library,* trans. Sir James George Frazer (Cambridge, MA: Harvard University Press; London: William Heinemann Ltd., 1921), 1.7.1.

2. Donald Richardson, *Great Zeus and All His Children* (Englewood Cliffs, NJ: Prentice-Hall, Inc., 1984), pp. 22–23.

3. Hesiod, *Works And Days,* translated by Hugh G. Evelyn-White, 69–82. http://www.sacred-texts.com/cla/hesiod/works.htm.

4. Hesiod, *Theogony* translated by Hugh G. Evelyn-White (ll. 507–543). http://www.sacred-texts.com/cla/hesiod/theogony.htm

5. Robert Graves, *Greek Gods and Heroes* (New York: Dell Publishing, 1960), p. 27.

6. Hesiod, *Theogony,* ll. 507–543.

7. H.A. Guerber, *The Myths of Greece and Rome* (New York: London House & Maxwell, 1963), p. 86.

8. Hesiod, *Theogony,* 929a–929t.

9. Graves, p. 15.

10. Ibid., p. 87.

11. Edith Hamilton, *Mythology* (Boston: Little, Brown and Company, 1969), p. 37.

12. Apollodorus, 3.14.6.

13. Hesiod: *Works And Days,* lines 373–375.

Chapter 4. A Wedding but No Marriage

1. Hesiod, *Theogony* translated by Hugh G. Evelyn-White, lines 176–206. http://www.sacred-texts.com/cla/hesiod/theogony.htm

2. Apollodorus, *The Library,* trans. Sir James George Frazer (Cambridge, MA: Harvard University Press; London: William Heinemann Ltd., 1921), 3.6.

3. Donald Richardson, *Great Zeus and All His Children* (Englewood Cliffs, NJ: Prentice-Hall, Inc., 1984), pp. 23–24.

4. Homer, *Iliad,* translated by Robert Fagles (New York: Penguin Putnam, 1990), Book 18, line 508.

5. "Limnos Island," http://www.thegreektravel.com/limnos/

Chapter 5. Armor for Achilles

1. Donald Richardson, *Great Zeus and All His Children* (Englewood Cliffs, NJ: Prentice-Hall, Inc., 1984), p. 25.

2. Homer, *Iliad,* translated by Robert Fagles (New York: Penguin Putnam, 1990), Book 19, lines 19–20.

3. Ibid., Book 21, lines. 260 ff.

4. Ibid., lines 389–392, 410–412, 415–416.

5. Homer, *Odyssey,* translated by Robert Fagles (New York: Penguin Putnam, 1996), Book 24, lines 75 ff.

6. Homer, *Iliad,* Book 20, lines 318–320.

7. Vergil, *Aeneid,* translated by Patric Dickinson (New York: New American Library, 1961), Book 8, lines 976–977.

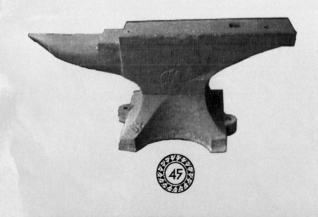

For Young Adults

Daly, Kathleen. *Greek and Roman Mythology A to Z*. New York: Facts on File, 2003.

Hamby, Zachary. *Mythology for Teens: Classic Myths for Today's World*. Austin, TX: Prufrock Press, 2009.

Houle, Michelle. *Gods and Goddesses in Greek Mythology*. Berkeley Heights, NJ: Enslow Publishers, 2001.

Oh Young Jin, Cirro. *Greek and Roman Mythology*. Singapore: Singapore Pte. Ltd., 2005.

Verniero, Joan. *An Illustrated Treasury of Read-Aloud Myths and Legends*. New York: Black Dog & Leventhal Publishers, 2004.

Works Consulted

Apollodorus. *The Library*. Translated by Sir James George Frazer. Cambridge, MA, Harvard University Press; London, William Heinemann Ltd., 1921.

Graves, Robert. *Greek Gods and Heroes*. New York: Dell Publishing, 1960.

Graves, Robert. *The Greek Myths,* Vol. I. New York: Penguin Books, 1977.

Guerber, H.A. *The Myths of Greece and Rome*. New York: London House & Maxwell, 1963.

Hamilton, Edith. *Mythology*. Boston: Little, Brown and Company, 1969.

Harshaw, Ruth. *The Council of the Gods*. Chicago: Thomas S. Rockwell Co, 1931.

Hesiod. *Theogony*.Translated by Hugh G. Evelyn-White, 1914. http://www.sacred-texts.com/cla/hesiod/theogony.htm

Hesiod: *Works And Days*. Translated by Hugh G. Evelyn-White, 1914. http://www.sacred-texts.com/cla/hesiod/works.htm

Holy Bible. King James Version.

Homeric Hymn 3 to Pythian Apollo. Translated by Evelyn-White, H G. Cambridge, MA: Harvard University Press, 1914. http://www.theoi.com/Text/HomericHymns1.html

Homer. *Iliad*. Translated by Robert Fagles. New York: Penguin Putnam, 1990.

Homer. *Odyssey*. Translated by Robert Fagles. New York: Penguin Putnam, 1996.

March, Jenny. *Cassell's Dictionary of Classical Mythology*. London: Cassell & Co., 2001.

Richardson, Donald. *Great Zeus and All His Children*. Englewood Cliffs, NJ: Prentice-Hall, Inc., 1984.

Richardson, Donald. *Greek Mythology for Everyone: Legends of the Gods and Heroes*. New York: Avenel Books, 1989.

Schwab, Gustav. *Gods and Heroes: Myths and Epics of Ancient Greece*. New York: Pantheon Books, Inc., 1957.

Stapleton, Michael. *The Illustrated Dictionary of Greek and Roman Mythology*. New York: Peter Bedrick Books, 1986.

Vergil. *Aeneid*. Translated by Patric Dickinson. New York: New American Library, 1961.

FURTHER READING

On the Internet
Ancient Greece for Kids. http://greece.mrdonn.org/index.html
Greek Mythology. http://www.mythweb.com/
Mythology Links: http://www.rcs.k12.va.us/csjh/mytholog.htm

GLOSSARY

allegory (AL-ih-gor-ee)—A story or painting that uses symbols to stand for another story or purpose.

anvil (AN-vil)—A heavy iron block against which a blacksmith hammers hot metal into desired shapes.

architecture (AR-kih-tek-cher)—The design of buildings.

astronomy (uh-STRAH-nuh-mee)—The science of studying stars and other objects in the universe.

bellow (BEL-oh)—A pump that a blacksmith uses to force air on a fire in a forge.

conspiracy (kun-SPEER-uh-see)—A secret plan, often for evil purposes.

courier (KUR-ee-er)—A messenger who travels quickly.

cuirass (KWEE-ras)—Armor worn on a soldier's trunk, usually made of leather.

Cyclops (SY-klops)—One of the race of giants with a single eye in the middle of the forehead. These giants were good at making weapons and using them in battle. The plural is *Cyclopes* (sy-kloh-PEEZ).

dowry (DOW-ree)—Items a girl's family gives to her husband, usually when the couple marries.

equanimity (ee-kwuh-NIH-mih-tee)—Calmness.

girdle (GUR-dul)—A belt or cord worn around the waist.

greaves (GREEVZ)—Leg armor worn below the knee.

grotto (GRAH-toh)—A cave or cavern.

impetuous (im-PET-choo-us)—Impulsive.

navigation (nah-vih-GAY-shun)—The art or science of plotting a course, as that of a ship.

passel (PAS-ul)—A group.

wrath (RATH)—Strong, stern, or fierce anger.